The Magic of Bermuda

CONTENTS

Dear Reader,
Welcome to the first edition of
Magic of Bermuda.

On behalf of the Ministry of Tourism & Transport and the people of Bermuda, I invite you to enjoy this wonderful publication, which truly captures the essence of our island home. In these vivid and vibrant photographs, you'll get a taste of Bermuda's natural beauty – our azure water, pink sand beaches and bright orange sunsets, as well as our friendly local people. They clearly show why Bermuda has often been referred to as the 'Jewel of the Atlantic'.

In the pages of this publication, you will discover the charm of our 54-square-kilometre (21-square-mile) island, with its two-lane roads, sorbet-coloured cottages, lush green golf courses, and our Bermuda shorts-clad business-men. For those who are keen on historical and cultural links, witness some of our most revered treasures, such as the Old Town of St. George's – a UNESCO World Heritage Site – as well as the historical shipyard of the Royal Naval Dockyard. And don't forget Bermuda's crystal-clear waters, which welcome swimmers, snorkellers and divers to a veritable wonderland of aquatic treasures.

Located a mere two hours from most major East Coast gateway cities and seven hours from the United Kingdom and Europe, Bermuda's proximity makes it easy to experience paradise. I am confident that once you have finished exploring the pages of this publication, you will be inspired to experience Bermuda first hand, and I invite you to come and sample what we have to offer our visitors.

Once again, I want to express my great pleasure that you have chosen to add this book to your collection, and I hope that its pages will fill you with warm memories of Bermuda and a desire to experience the magnificence of our island again and again.

Sincerely,

Dr. The Hon. Ewart F. Brown, JP, MP;   The Minister of Tourism & Transport

Above left A Parliamentary Democracy, the seat of Bermuda's Government has been housed in this dignified building, in Hamilton, for almost two centuries.

Below left Bermuda has 103km (64 miles) of coastline.

Above The Annual Cup Match Classic is a major sporting and social event. Cricket teams from Somerset and St.George's play each other in a two-day sporting fiesta.

Right Named for Sir Thomas Gates, Lt. Governor of Virginia, who was aboard the Sea Venture when it was wrecked here in 1609, this 17th century fort marks the entrance into St. George's Harbour.

THE ISLANDS OF BERMUDA

There are many things about Bermuda that make it truly unique. Perhaps most remarkable is the fact that this cluster of islands remained quite unknown to the rest of the world until the dawn of the 16th century, when it was sighted by the crew of a passing Spanish galleon. Subsequent shipwrecks confirmed that there were no inhabitants.

After the islands were colonized, it was established that Bermuda owed its isolated origin to the eruptions of volcanoes, whose eroded peaks were washed by the warm coral-laden

Opposite A popular anchorage for local boaters, delightful Flatts Village has its roots in a 17th century fishing community. Today, there are shops, several small eateries and also the Bermuda Government Aquarium.

Above Secluded beaches such as this one at Ely's Harbour can always be discovered by boaters.

Left Bermuda shorts were invented at the turn of the 20th century in London, England. They are the national dress for Bermuda and should be worn three inches above the knee, accompanied by Bermuda hose (long white socks) and loafers with tassels.

Above With beds of sea grass and coral outcrops close to shore, Clearwater Beach is popular with swimmers, snorkellers and picnickers.

Left An outstanding example of 19th century Bermudian neo-classical architecture, Camden sits in the grounds of the Botanical Gardens and it is the official residence of the Premier. In the rear, a converted Arrowroot Factory accommodates the Masterworks Collection of Bermuda artwork.

Opposite top St David's — once an island but now connected to the mainland — was named by a Welsh colonist after his nation's patron saint.

waters of the Gulf Stream. Reefs grew and were in turn shattered into the sandy particles that, in time, created the current landforms. Once entirely hidden in the mid-Atlantic, Bermuda had mysteriously emerged from beneath the sea, unseen.

The permanent proximity of the Gulf Stream produces not only the world's most northern living coral reef but also a humid subtropical climate. The combined result is miles of beaches with a pinkish glow, and lush vegetation characterized by a year-round profusion of exotic flowers. There are no conventional seasons. Bermuda is far from the polluted continents and generates

Right Whitewashed roofs are one of Bermuda's most characteristic features.

Left The sun sets on another beautiful day in Bermuda.

Above An annual highlight in the Governor's calendar, The Peppercorn Ceremony marks the occasion when a local Lodge pays the Bermuda Government its yearly rent of one peppercorn, for use of the seventeenth century State House.

Right This unique church was constructed in 1827, during the hours of darkness, by a group of neighbourhood slaves.

virtually no pollution of its own and thus the air is refreshingly clean and pure. On a clear day, there truly is a sense that one can see forever and the turquoise waters are so unclouded that colourful fish can always be spotted feeding along the docks and shoreline.

Bermudians themselves are also distinct. Because this untouched island group had no indigenous peoples, all Bermudians are descended from successive waves of various immigrants, primarily from Africa and Europe. Today they live in a small, comfortable community atmosphere where cordiality remains alive and well. Bermudians have time to say 'Thank you!' to the bus driver, instinctively greet one another with 'Hello!' and 'Good morning!' and can even get a trifle ruffled if they receive no reply.

Whether one is strolling the narrow roadways, scuba-diving a wreck or simply sitting on the rocks and gazing out to sea, Bermuda presents a timeless mood of tranquility, which many say is simply magical.

LOCATION AND GEOGRAPHY

Bermuda is located in the western Atlantic Ocean, at 32 degrees north and 64 degrees west. This mid-ocean group of islands lies approximately 1050km (650 miles) off the eastern seaboard of North America, and with the West Indies about 1700km (1050 miles) to the south and North Africa 4800km (2980 miles) due east, it is isolated and peaceful.

In general terms, Bermuda is perched atop an extinct volcano that is ringed by a coral reef.

Geologists estimate that approximately one million years ago lava burst from the bed of the Atlantic some three kilometres (two miles) below sea level and blasted its way towards the surface, eventually leaving a submerged range of several volcanic peaks. As the sea gradually calmed and the cones became cool, coral polyps borne by the Gulf Stream were washed among the remnant rims, and colonies of these tiny marine creatures attached themselves around the sides. Over time, the skeletal remains of successive generations created the atoll-like reefs that completely encircle Bermuda to this day.

Persistent wave action has continuously eroded these reefs, reducing both the coral and a myriad of companion seashells to tiny fragments. When washed ashore, this sand produced Bermuda's distinctive pink-flecked beaches; when wind-borne, it accumulated

Above left Bermuda's first bank, created by N.T.Butterfield in the 19th century. This institution has now expanded into the global marketplace.

Left The Government Ferry Terminal in Hamilton provides commuters and sightseeing visitors with efficient, comfortable and easy access to most parts of the country.

Opposite The remnants of 17th century fortifications are found scattered throughout the islands. The fort on Castle Island was designed to protect Bermuda's Eastern coastline.

as sand dunes. The present undulating landscape represents the fossilized remains of those original dunes, whose present form has been modified by the wind and rain and then elegantly draped with layers of subtropical vegetation. The original coastline was dramatically sculpted by changing interglacial sea levels and the contemporary shores are heavily indented as a result of both wave action and seasonal storms. The combined impact of these elements has left an abundance of coves and cliff faces, interspersed with numerous beaches.

CLIMATE

Although geographically situated well beyond the range of the true Tropics, Bermuda enjoys a very pleasing subtropical climate throughout the year. This is largely thanks to its proximity to the Gulf Stream, an ocean 'river' that flows through this portion of the Atlantic with decidedly warmer waters than might otherwise be expected this far north. Originating near the Equator, the Gulf Stream reaches Bermuda accompanied by its own adjacent bodies of warm air and the islands become the prime beneficiaries.

Bermuda's annual summertime temperatures remain steadily around 30°C (86°F) without the benefit of significant diurnal variations. At the opposite end of the climatic scale, they may drop to around 16°C (61°F) in February. However, the temperature plays a less significant role in the daily lives of locals and visitors than does humidity. Bermuda has a damp climate with an average daily relative humidity of 78 per cent, but humidity levels are constantly higher than this – day and night alike – between May and October, providing an environment that those from northern climes invariably liken to that within a greenhouse.

Rainfall, upon which Bermudians rely almost exclusively for their drinking water, is fairly evenly spread throughout the year. Total annual rainfall is around 150–65cm (59–65in), which means that islanders have become natural masters at water conservation. It rains on average 183 days per year, but these downpours frequently come as short sharp tropical showers. In summer they typically burst from a clear blue cloudless sky, last for a few minutes and then are gone again. Bermudians appreciate the rainfall not only because it fills their water tanks, but also as a vital provider for the lush vegetation that dominates the landscape

Above Traffic policemen in Bermuda will be happy to point lost tourists in the right direction.

Below Travelling by ferry is a great way to avoid road traffic; the journey is relaxing and the scenery unrivalled.

Opposite There are many delicious fish available in Bermuda restaurants. Fish Chowder is a popular dish.

ECONOMY

Reliant upon outside sources for most of its domestic needs, Bermuda's economy is curiously fragile yet robust. The island has no significant manufacturing industries and the vast majority of its goods are imported on cargo ships that arrive regularly two or three times each week. Even homegrown produce is insufficient to meet demand and is supplemented by overseas suppliers.

Nevertheless, Bermuda is one of the richest countries in the world, enjoying a high per capita income and negligible unemployment. This healthy situation has been accomplished by careful management of an economy that is based on two main pillars: tourism and international business.

Attracted partly by its close proximity to North America, visitors can discover a relaxed alternative lifestyle just a couple of hours away by plane. An average of 250,000 visitors fly here each year, while another 200,000 arrive by cruise ships. For the vast majority, these islands truly are another world, offering an escape from the stressful, overcrowded and frequently polluted cities scattered along the northeastern seaboard of the USA. With their year-round subtropical climate, the islands of Bermuda are also particularly alluring to those wanting relief from a harsh continental winter.

A high percentage of local jobs are directly and indirectly related to tourism. Others in the workforce are involved in the second pillar of Bermuda's economy, international business. Spanning the full spectrum from reinsurance and global banking to investments, trade and commerce, there are over 12,000 companies registered in Bermuda, most of which have their active headquarters in Hamilton, the capital.

Very sensitive to its reputation as a centre for international business, the Bermudian Government has always consciously sought to cultivate openess and honesty as hallmarks

Opposite The City of Hamilton, a port city, is the capital and administrative, commercial, entertainment and shopping center of Bermuda. It is named after Henry Hamilton, who was appointed by King George III of Britain as 'our Lieutenant Governor of our islands of Bermuda (or Somers Isles) in America, and Commander in Chief of our Forts called King's Castle, Fort Hamilton, Fort Popple and Fort Paget' on February 26, 1787.

Right Fanny Fox Cottage is an authentic example of 18th century Bermudian architecture, nestled in the tranquil residential district of St.George's.

Below left and right St.George's has been designated a 'World Heritage Site' by the United Nations. Narrow lanes meander through residential neighbourhoods of original homes that were constructed by Bermuda's earliest settlers.

for all transactions. Reviews by European and world overseers have consistently confirmed a high moral reputation.

All monetary activities – local, foreign and government alike – are regulated through the offices of the Bermuda Monetary Authority. This organization is empowered to issue and redeem Bermudian currency, oversee and advise all locally based financial institutions, detect and prevent financial crime, manage exchange controls and ensure the constant application of related legislation. In effect, the BMA is the guardian of Bermuda's financial integrity and is, in turn, audited by the Auditor-General. Such careful monitoring has helped to keep Bermuda's economy on a firm footing.

From the 16th Century to the Present Day

At the dawn of the 16th century, Spanish sailor Juan de Bermudez declared himself to be the discoverer of Bermuda. Although an exact date is difficult to pinpoint – historians generally accept it to have been around 1505 – the earliest maps drawn by Peter Martyr and Gonzales Oviedo certainly date the islands' discovery before 1510.

Above Her Majesty Queen Elizabeth II's official birthday is celebrated in Bermuda with a formal military parade, led by His Excellency the Governor and Bermuda Premier.

Left St Peter's is the oldest continuously-used Anglican church in the so-called New World. With sections dating back to the 17th century, the current building stands on the site of the original structure. The use of cedar throughout is typical of its period.

Opposite above The Martello Tower along Ferry Reach was constructed in 1823 and was initially built as part of the defences deemed necessary to repel a possible invasion by American forces during the Revolutionary War. It remains in an outstanding state of preservation.

UNCOMMON HISTORIC BEGINNINGS

Before 1510, there had been only myths and rumours to suggest that somewhere deep in mid-Atlantic there lay a mysterious group of enchanted islands. Even the mighty Chinese fleet of 1421–3, which mapped most of the world, including the Caribbean and the eastern seaboard from Florida northwards to Greenland, failed to see Bermuda. Strangely enough, Bermudez apparently never landed here. Considerably more interested in the gold and silver bullion that lay waiting in Central and South America, he soon determined that these unpopulated islands offered nothing to plunder and quickly headed south.

Astonishingly, despite several shipwrecks, the islands of Bermuda remained uninhabited for a further century.

In 1609, however, a fleet of nine vessels set sail from England bound for Jamestown, Virginia. Established by the Virginia Company in 1607, the population of that fledgling American colony had become so critically reduced by a combination of disease and starvation that a relief fleet was dispatched. From the original convoy, only five ships were destined to survive this disastrous journey.

Soon after the fleet entered the deep

Right The Salvation Army church in Bermuda has actively contributed to social services for the needy since its inception.

Left Built by the British Navy in the 19th century, the Clocktower building at The Royal Navy Dockyard has been now sensitively converted into an unusual shopping mall. The Government ferry system provides a leisurely link into Hamilton.

Below The Bermuda College offers students technical and academic courses leading to a two-year Associate's Degree. Credit Transfers to several overseas institutions can also be arranged.

Atlantic, a major storm developed – a succession of violent depressions rather than just a single event. Tempestuous conditions prevailed for several weeks, during which time two boats returned to the safety of England and another sank with all hands. The flagship of this tormented fleet was *Sea Venture*, captained by the distinguished Christopher Newport. Alongside him stood Sir George Somers, Admiral of the beleaguered flotilla. Engulfed by unrelenting, deteriorating conditions, *Sea Venture* was severely battered and gradually began to disintegrate. As passengers and crew hopelessly bailed, a sense of helplessness steadily took hold of them – they were sinking.

On the brink of that awesome inevitability, land was sighted and they were miraculously shipwrecked on the eastern shores of Bermuda. (The story of this extraordinary event and its aftermath were subsequently immortalized by William Shakespeare in his play *The Tempest*.) Marooned here for ten months, the survivors built two boats from the wreckage of their ship, supplemented by locally found Bermuda cedar, and eventually sailed for Jamestown. Following their unsought sojourn, the immigrants were delivered to Virginia and the crew returned to England. However,

the enthusiasm of the survivors convinced the shareholders of the Virginia Company that Bermuda should be colonized. Consequently, in 1612, as a direct result of the shipwrecking of the *Sea Venture*, the first settlers dropped anchor in St George's Harbour. The human colonization of these islands had begun.

Opposite top First put into service in 1879, Gibb's Hill Lighthouse is the more powerful of Bermuda's two lighthouses. It is used by shipping to locate this isolated destination, out here in the heart of the Atlantic Ocean.

Opposite bottom The Gothic elegance of The Cathedral of the Most Holy Trinity, Hamilton.

GROWTH AND DEVELOPMENT

As the first nucleated settlement, St George's became Bermuda's original capital – a mantle that it was destined to hold until 1815, when, for centralization purposes, Hamilton assumed this responsibility. Although secondary communities developed around the inlet at Flatts, as well as at Elys Harbour and Somerset in the West End, it was in and around this East End seaport that the islands were initially developed. The first stone houses were erected here and the embryo of an economy started to evolve, based primarily upon shipbuilding, agriculture and fishing.

As if sensing a need to justify being here, the early settlers sought to create a diverse economy involving an export trade. They tried pearl diving, planted tobacco and mulberry bushes and imported silk worms in the hope of stimulating a local silk industry. Unfortunately, all such efforts proved fruitless. Instead, during the 18th century, as Bermuda's mid-Atlantic location became firmly established, its ports became increasingly important for ship repairs, entrepreneur trading and a variety of similar maritime-related activities.

By the dawn of the 19th century it had become evident that one of Bermuda's most significant attributes lay in its strategic location – a benefit originally recognized by the survivors of the *Sea Venture* shipwreck. From this mid-Atlantic position, the entire western ocean could be patrolled and monitored. The English subsequently established a Royal Naval Dockyard at Ireland Island and the army quickly followed suit by constructing full garrisons at St George and on the outskirts of Hamilton. English warships had reaped strategic benefits from the American Revolutionary War of 1775 and now merchant vessels gained remarkable financial rewards during the American Civil War of 1861–5. In a like manner, each of these military facilities proved itself abundantly beneficial during the two World Wars – and in the 1960s Bermuda played a key role throughout the Cuban Missile Crisis.

By the 1940s, the Canadian and US governments had also contracted to establish military presences here, ones that would thrive throughout the Cold

War Era. In the early years of manned space flight, NASA constructed a tracking centre at Cooper's Island, in St George's Parish, and from here all rocket launches were monitored for the next 30 years. Computers at Cooper's Island were the first earthly receptors to receive data beamed from transmitters landed on the moon. The advance of technology eventually made these facilities redundant by the end of the twentieth century and their leased properties were duly returned to the Bermuda Government.

Bermuda's strategic location has played a significant part throughout its history. Today, it is a world leader in the fields of international communications, global finance, insurance and tourism.

POPULATION

Although Bermuda's workforce can boast a diversity of nationalities from throughout the world, its own population is based primarily upon three distinct groups. Approximately 64,000 Bermudians inhabit these islands. Of these, census returns reveal that 61 per cent are of African descent and 39 per cent are classified as 'white', the majority of whom are of European

Opposite top The gentility of a traditional carriage ride awaits visitors arriving aboard an ultra-modern cruise-ship.

Opposite bottom The port of Hamilton thrives on shipping activity. However, this city is also the focal-point of Bermuda's international business community.

Above Regular daily flights link Bermuda's ocean front International Airport with North America and Europe.

Right Sitting atop a hillside on the outskirts of Hamilton, Government House is an imposing 19th century structure. The residence of the Governor is also used as a social venue for entertaining local and visiting dignitaries, as well as the traditional Queen's Birthday garden party.

extraction. Within this latter category there is a notable Portuguese component – the ancestors of those who were brought here from the Azores after 1847 to work as land labourers.

The vast majority of black Bermudians can trace their ancestry back to the West Indies, from where most were bought as slaves during the 17th and 18th centuries. It is interesting to note that the first two 'people of

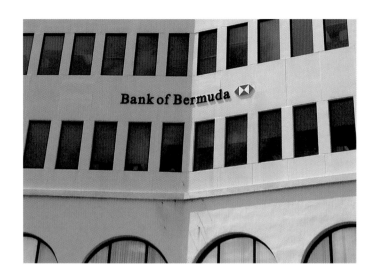

Above left The Bank of Bermuda, a recent member of the HSBC Group, has affiliations and subsidiaries world-wide.

Above right This whitewashed cottage is a typical example of colonial architecture. The lush garden is a product of the subtropical climate.

Opposite Set amidst well-groomed grounds at the West End, popular Cambridge Beaches offers its guests individual self-contained suites accompanied by first class service.

Below Bermuda's oldest port in the town of St.George's accommodates international cruise ships at its modern terminal on Ordnance Island.

Page 24, top Waterloo House on Pitts' Bay Road nestles along the Hamilton waterfront. Formerly an 18th century home, it has been tastefully converted and is now an extremely elegant hotel with one of the best restaurants on the island.

colour' to land here had nothing to do with slavery, but came to Bermuda in 1616 as pearl divers. Although their efforts produced limited results, they remained on the islands. By the time that slavery was legally abolished in August 1834, the official register listed a total of 4177 slaves, the majority of whom were born in Bermuda. There were an additional 250 'coloureds', who had already secured their freedom and were living productive lives of their own. Today, more accurately reflecting the true population balance, black Bermudians are deeply involved in all aspects of trade, commerce, education and politics.

Many white Bermudian families justifiably boast of being descended from those settlers who arrived from England during the decades following the arrival of *The Plough* in 1612. Historically, their roles became those of business and political leaders. Such social and economic functions did not generally begin to percolate throughout the population until the 20th century but are now broadly shared by the whole community.

Members of the Portuguese community traditionally established themselves in farming and

Below The efficient government transportation system enables visitors and residents to travel throughout Bermuda, whilst enjoying the scenery with air-conditioned comfort.

Opposite top The lighthouse on St.David's Island is used as a beacon to direct incoming and departing ships and yachts through the complicated reef pattern, and helps to guide them into the relative safety of the eastern channel.

Opposite bottom Frances Patton School is a Government Primary School, built on a hillside overlooking the waters of the North Shore.

gardening activities. Now, although freely dispersed among all employment aspects of the island's economy, many still work in areas associated with agriculture, landscaping and Government Parks.

Bermuda's economic workforce is augmented by 'guest workers', who come from around the globe. On the whole, they are engaged in areas of employment where insufficient locals are available to fill all of the vacancies and can often be found in areas related to finance, accountancy, law, international business, banking and reinsurance.

SYSTEM OF GOVERNMENT

Bermuda is a parliamentary democracy, in which the local electorate votes for its own political leaders on the basis of one member to represent each of 36 constitutionally established constituencies. The leader of the party holding the majority of the seats in parliament, with the approval of the party itself, becomes the country's premier. With that position also comes the right to appoint a ministerial cabinet.

Since the mid-1960s, the political landscape has been dominated by two major parties: the Progressive Labour Party and the United Bermuda Party. New elections must be called before the expiration of a continuous five-year term in office.

Ever since the Constitutional Conference of 1967, Bermuda has been a semi-autonomous territory within the British Commonwealth.

Although Bermuda is substantially responsible for the majority of its own affairs, a Governor is appointed to represent the Queen. This role is designed to serve as a direct link to Buckingham Palace and Westminster, but it also bestows upon the office-holder full responsibility for the island's defence and internal security. The Governor is also expected to ensure the integrity of the judiciary.

EDUCATION

With a very high cost of living, accompanied by an equally high standard of living, Bermudians are generally well-travelled, conversationally worldly and, on the whole, relatively sophisticated. Such characteristics are partially the result of constant direct contact with visitors and guest workers from all around the world, but are also the natural outgrowth of a system that provides free primary and secondary school education for every child. The long-established practice of wearing school uniform cultivates a sense of both group and personal pride. Within government and private schools alike, students are encouraged to participate in both local and international certificates of academic achievement. Upon completion of these, the Bermuda College is available for those who may wish to earn local qualifications or secure academic credits that may be applied towards certain overseas university programmes. Others may leave secondary school and enter undergraduate studies in Canada, the USA or the United Kingdom.

Within Bermuda, many specialist institutions and associations are available to assist young Bermudians interested in directly pursuing careers in such diverse fields as law, architecture, nursing, banking and accountancy and there are many scholarships, awards and loan-assistance programmes, enabling most individuals to follow their dreams.

Opposite top A fisherman returns to shore after spending the day travelling among the inner and outer reefs.

Opposite bottom Painters restore the customary whiteness to a Bermuda home. The roof has been the principle source of catching fresh rainwater since the 17th century.

Above left One of several private schools, Saltus Grammar School provides a broad-based academic programme that leads many graduates towards overseas universities.

Above right Ordnance Island is a man-made island in St George's Parish, although it is now permanently connected to St. George's by a bridge. It was a US Navy submarine base when, two years after the British, the USA entered World War II.

Right An enterprising, and relaxed Bermudan sells his daily catch. Rockfish and Snapper are two of the most popular fish served in homes and restaurants on the islands.

Above left Elbow Beach Hotel is a full resort facility, catering to individual visitors and conventions. With its own beach, several restaurants and shops, all guest rooms overlook the ocean.

Above right Perched atop an ancient fortification, Harbour Radio is the main telecommunications centre for all sea traffic arriving and departing from Bermuda.

Above Castle island is home to the Captain's House, built in 1621. It is said to be the oldest standing stone home in the Northern Hemisphere.

Left Located along the picturesque South Shore, Ariel Sands is a typical cottage colony, where guests have their own self-contained units overlooking the sea.

Opposite left The Fairmont Hamilton Princess Hotel is located conveniently within easy walking distance to the centre of Hamilton. A complimentary transit service links it to its sister hotel in Southampton Parish.

Opposite right Many varieties of fruit and vegetables grow on the islands. Here, some fresh produce is carefully prepared by one of Bermuda's trained chefs.

Right Converted from a century-old private residence, Rosedon offers first class accommodation and dining facilities, with very personal attention, close to the heart of Hamilton.

Below The introduction of a convenient and comfortable system of fast ferries has made most parts of Bermuda readily accessible by water transport.

Left The elegant Commissioner's House oversees not only the entire Naval Dockyard complex, but also commands imposing views of the main shipping channels.

Below The 19th century Anglican cathedral dominates the Hamilton skyline.

Flora and Fauna

Before the arrival of people, Bermuda's natural landscape was dominated by a vast forest of cedar and palmetto. Scattered in its midst were delicate snowberry shrubs and along the shoreline were stands of bay grape, the yellow blooms of coastal sophora and prickly pear cacti. Over time, human encroachment has significantly decimated this endemic flora. However, Bermudians remain constantly aware of the visual and psychological benefits of being surrounded by healthy vegetation and plant bushes, trees and ornamental plants to enrich their natural surroundings.

FLORA

The island's roadways are lined with pink oleander hedgerows interspersed with the multicoloured blooms of hibiscus, which are among the many introduced species that flourish in this subtropical climate. Poinsettias thrive outdoors and even dutifully turn red, pink or white just in time for Christmas. Tall orange and yellow poincianas sweep majestically over houses

and main roads, as do creamy magnolias, flame trees, bougainvillea and scarlet cordia. Along walking trails, the fragrances from frangipani and white Japanese pittisporum mingle freely with allspice and honeysuckle.

The pawpaw tree – distinctive with its slender trunk, broad leaves and clusters of green fruit – is so abundant here that some gardeners regard it as a weed. They may also view geraniums and nasturtiums in the same way. Citrus trees are common in many gardens, providing oranges, lemons, limes and grapefruits for local consumption. Bananas were first introduced into Bermuda as early as 1616 and proved to be so easy to propagate that they quickly spread throughout the islands. Loquats, Surinam cherries and avocados similarly prosper in this mid-Atlantic haven.

Bereft of conventional seasons, Bermuda's natural landscape is a colourful delight all year long. The Botanical Gardens, centrally located in Paget Parish, house the Government's official collection of trees, shrubs, bushes and cacti.

Page 32, top Perhaps the most exotic of flowers, hibiscus hedgerows thrive in the Bermuda climate and come in a variety of colours from deep red through to white and yellow.

Page 32, bottom Introduced into these islands a century ago, hibiscus of all colours have rapidly established themselves among roadside hedges and in private gardens.

Page 33 Bougainvillea becomes a common sight during much of May through to July.

Opposite top This quiet lane is edged by oleanders, with an endemic cedar tree on the left. Severely decimated by a mid-twentieth century blight, a replanting programme is underway.

Opposite bottom The finest selection of Bermuda-grown variety of Easter Lilies are traditionally sent to Queen Elizabeth II.

Above The blooms of Pittisporum exude a sweet fragrance around each plant. Their leaves do well in a salty environment.

Above The delicate Bermudiana is unofficially regarded as the National Flower. It flourishes in lawns and along the roadsides.

Right The spiked Yucca plant grows abundantly among the sand-dunes along the South Shore.

Page 38 Poinsettia trees grow in the wild in Bermuda, where the common red variety may reach heights of 4 metres (12 foot). Here, the cultivated versions are being grown commercially so that they are at their best just in time for the festive season.

FAUNA

Although covering an area of just 54-square-kilometres (21-square-miles), Bermuda has two endemic species of wildlife registered on the IUCN (International Union for Conservation of Nature and Natural Resources) Red List of Threatened Species. Unquestionably, the most celebrated of these is the cahow, a member of the petrel family that was long believed to have become extinct. When the first settlers arrived, they found this native bird to be an immediate food source and soon had decimated its numbers to a critical level. By the latter part of the nineteenth century, the cahow, also known as the Bermuda petrel, was officially designated as 'extinct'. It remained so until the mid-twentieth century, when isolated carcasses were discovered and, finally, individual live birds were identified. Probably the most protected bird on the planet, the cahow, after 50 years of careful supervision and management, has gradually become tentatively re-established to the extent that just over 200 individuals are known to exist. Their nesting sites continue to be familiar to only a chosen few. A nocturnal bird, it is rarely seen over the land – even by the most avid of ornithologists – although recently sightings have been confirmed out at sea.

The second 'Bermudian' on the endangered species list is the somewhat less flamboyant rock lizard, or Bermuda skink. This is an endemic chameleon whose population has been dev-

astated by both human encroachment and the introduction of various predators. Ongoing research, encouraged by the Bermuda Zoological Society, has now successfully identified pockets of surviving skinks and a breeding programme has been introduced. Unlike others of this genus, the Bermuda skink has a scaly skin and prefers a rocky coastal habitat with lots of shade.

Aside from these two very special species, Bermuda is a wonderful place for watching birds and fish. Bird watchers will be interested to know that these islands have 22 residents, with an annual checklist that expands to just over 360 species when vagrants and transients are counted. Herons frequent the mangroves; cattle egrets are commonly found in farmlands, while ruddy turnstones and sandpipers are regular scavengers among the seaweed and beaches. Red cardinals, yellow-breasted kiskadees and bluebirds are also very common. The bird most frequently associated with Bermuda is the longtail. These elegant cliff-dwellers are regarded as the harbingers of spring, and when they finally head back to the ocean with their fledglings in late August, schoolchildren seem to sense that their own holidays are quietly coming to a close.

Inevitably, Bermuda has always had a close affinity with the sea and all those creatures that live within it. Gazing into the crystal waters from the rocks, or glancing down from a bridge, visitors soon become as fascinated and absorbed as Bermudians themselves by the abundance of sea life that can be seen. Parrotfish, angelfish, miscellaneous wrasse, bream, grunt, garfish, cow pollies and squirrelfish are all there in profusion. Just below the surface are groups of squid, lurking on the edge of a school of thousands of tiny leaping fry; on the sandy bottom are sea slugs and spiny urchins. Actually, all of these can also be seen in air-conditioned comfort at the Bermuda Aquarium, Museum and Zoo, located in Flatts, where visitors can also watch local sharks, moray eels, groupers, octopus and lobsters.

Research into the local maritime environment has enjoyed a long tradition. It was here, during the late 1920s, that Dr William Beebee huddled with engineer Otis Barton and commenced man's first descent into the darkness of the ocean. Together, they were lowered half a mile down into these ominous depths and became the first humans to see and verbally record the 'creatures and monsters' that others had only dared to speculate upon. Later, in the 1950s, the earliest sonic recordings of the 'song' of the humpback whale were made off Bermuda's South Shore. These mighty mammals continue to migrate through

Above The heart of the Sago Palm reveals clusters of peach-size seed pods.

Right When in full-bloom the tall and sprawling Poinciana Tree provides a radiant canopy above roads and gardens.

Top left An introduced species, the Kiskadee Flycatcher is now among the most common birds to be seen in Bermuda.

Top right and middle The botanical Gardens are a mix of park, woodland, greenhouses, agricultural buildings and horticultural collections.

Left Nonsuch island was acquired by the Bermuda Government in 1964, as part of its nature reserve, bird and wildlife system, through funds donated by the New York Zoological Society. Now the Nonsuch Island Nature Reserve is a living museum, a re-creation of Bermuda's native flora and fauna.

these waters during April and May each year.

Anyone interested in Bermuda's diverse environments will need to become familiar with the extraordinary project being undertaken at Nonsuch Island, in St George's Parish. Here, on an isolated island, an ongoing attempt is being made to restore Nonsuch to its natural, pre-colonial habitat. Non-endemic plants have been uprooted, while herons have been reintroduced, along with land crabs and skinks. Turtle eggs have again

been hatched on its beaches and the land has been substantially purged of introduced predators. The ultimate yardstick of success will be when cahows again return to build their nests among the cliffs. Visits to Nonsuch Island are meticulously monitored, but tours are sometimes arranged through the Bermuda Biological Station for Research, along Ferry Reach in St George's Parish.

Top The Longtail is a national symbol of Bermuda and many souvenirs feature its image. It is Bermuda's traditional harbinger of spring and is a beautiful sight along the coastline during the summer. The Longtail population has declined steadily due to increased development, pollution and pigeons competing for the same nests. There is presently a Longtail nesting site crisis, and in an attempt to solve the problem, Longtail 'igloos' were invented in the late 1990s to provide alternative nesting opportunities. These man-made structures are made from roofing material, which is light but strong, with a camouflaged concrete covering. They provide good insulation and shelter from the elements. So far 35 Longtail igloos are in place on Nonsuch Island and they appear to be popular with the birds.

Above One of the rarest birds on earth, the Cahow has been carefully brought back from presumed extinctio, to a meticulously protected population. There are now approximately 200 healthy individuals. When the first settlers arrived in Bermuda in the early 1600s it is thought that there were half a million cahows on the islands. Unfortunately they were so easy to catch and eat that they were hunted to presumed extinction. These nocturnal birds mate for life and the female lays a single egg each year.

Above left Flamingos are not native to Bermuda, but they can be seen at the Bermuda Aquarium.

Above right Chameleons abound everywhere, and are noted for changing their colour to that of their surroundings.

Left Bermuda is a sanctuary for dolphins, Humpback, Blue and Northern Whales due to its strict 320 kilometre (200 mile) exclusive fishing zone.

Above Tree frogs, or whistling frogs are nocturnal. They spend the night in trees and during the day hide under stones and leaves. The males 'sing' at night in order to attact mates.

Right Bufo Marinus is a large toad, whose nocturnal behaviour makes it a common sight on roadways and in gardens. They were imported into Bermuda from Guyana in 1875 in order to control cockroaches. Their main diet is insects but they also eat lizards, frogs, mice and even dog and cat food.

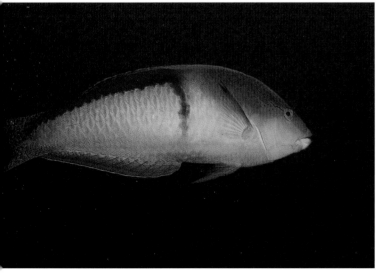

Opposite bottom Yellowhead Wrasse inhabit shallow reefs with exposed rocky ledges.

Opposite top left Spanish Hogfish are a deep red to purple colour on the upper-fore-body with a yellow head and belly. They feed on crustaceans, molluscs, and sea urchins.

Below The Bermuda Angelfish is a common sight when snorkelling or diving around the reefs. It can also be found on Bermuda's five cents coin.

Left The Spiny Lobster is found on many Bermuda restaurant menus from September to March. This lobster lacks large claws and is commonly found in holes and crevices at the bottom of the reef. Shy and secretive during the day, they venture out at night from their hiding places to feed on plants and small animals. In the shallow waters around Bermuda, they mate from mid-April to mid-May, and in June egg-bearing females go to deeper waters where they spawn. Each female releases 50,000 to 800,000 eggs.

Reefs, Beaches & Shipwrecks

Bermuda has several stunning beaches, both large and small. Tiny dark red skeletal animals that grow profusely on the underside of Bermuda's coral reefs form the basis of the sand on Bermuda's beaches, giving them the characteristic pink colour. Further into the water, Bermuda has more than 500 square kilometres (200 square miles) of coral reef, teeming with marine life, to explore, as well as several shipwrecks, which give the islands the name of 'Shipwreck Capital of the Atlantic'.

REEFS

Bermudians like to describe the configuration of their island as resembling a fishhook. Resting on a northwest–southeast angle, it is entirely surrounded by an elliptical-shaped reef that stretches about a kilometre from the South Shore and then arcs outwards approximately 13.5km (8½ miles) from the northernmost edge. At this point is North Rock, a portion of the reef that sits boldly exposed at low tide. Historically, this complicated network of coral reefs served as a natural defensive system against potential invaders. But it also serves to delineate the deep oceanic waters on the outside from the shallower inland waters.

Outside the reef swim the larger game fish and sharks. Marlin, tuna and bonita are the subjects of a robust sports-fishing industry, in which a tag-and-release policy has been in place for many years, primarily to protect marlin and sailfish. Occasionally whale sharks are sighted and, after being pho-

Above Some types of reef are known as 'boilers' because the continuous breaking of waves makes it look as if the sea is boiling.

Opposite Horseshoe Bay is one of Bermuda's most famous beaches. Sadly, it was extensively damaged during Hurricane Fabian in September 2003, after this picture was taken.

tographed, these remarkable 'gentle giants' are left to glide unhindered on their way. In late spring, pods of humpback whales breach the surface along the South Shore as they continue on their migratory pilgrimage northwards.

Inside and among the reefs, all manner of fish of different shapes, sizes and hues can be readily spotted, making Bermuda one of the most popular dive sites in this region for snorkellers and scuba divers alike. Fish such as grouper, rockfish, snappers and hind are eagerly sought by local commercial fishermen who sell them along the waterfront during most afternoons in Hamilton and St George. Many are bought by hotels and restaurants for use in famous Bermudian culinary dishes.

All of the living reefs are carefully protected from damage and destruction by a miscellany of laws and regulations, which strictly prohibit the gathering of such corals as well as many shellfish. Known fish-breeding areas are similarly designated off-limits to fishermen. Lobsters can be caught only during a specifically defined season and must conform to a 15cm (6in) tail length before they may be landed.

BEACHES

The overwhelming beauty of its beaches and coastline have made Bermuda one of the most photographed islands in the world. The adjacent waters fluctuate from clear crystal to turquoise and shades of cobalt blue in colour. From the air, this maritime scenery is so spectacular that even the most seasoned airline pilots will often provide an unscheduled lap of honour prior to adopting their final approach to landing.

Stretching intermittently for many miles, the majority of Bermuda's beaches unfold gently into the sea, either from the base of craggy limestone cliffs or from bulky sand dunes. Weathered by centuries of wind and sea erosion, the cliffs – which range in shade from grey to pale yellow and ochre – are naturally indented, their surfaces frequently jagged and sharp.

Among the crevices, the island's trademark longtails build their nests in spring and then remain permanent residents while they feed and rear their young. By late August they are ready to retreat once more to the open ocean for the

Above Whether riding a rented auxiliary cycle or sitting in a comfortable air-conditioned Government bus, travelling along the meandering coastal roadways, with their amazing views of the ocean, is always a pleasurable experience.

Opposite An isolated island off the East End of Bermuda, Nonsuch has been painstakingly restored to the same natural habitat that it originally enjoyed prior to human colonisation. As such, it is only accessible by private arrangement. During the late 1920's, Dr.William Beebee conducted his pioneering descents into the nearby ocean depths.

remainder of the year. They share their environment with lizards and crabs. Land crabs are quite prevalent, concealing themselves deep inside their sandy burrows among the dunes, but even more fascinating to watch are the nimble Sally Lightfoot crabs, which feed among the lapping waves while clinging precariously to the rocky outcrops. Their shells lying among the boulders may be evidence that the crabs have fallen prey to hungry herons, but more usually they will have been cast aside when their occupants have outgrown them.

The majority of the beaches line the South Shore. This is the geophysical aspect that benefits most from the dominant prevailing winds and ocean currents. During their journey towards land, the waves break tiny fragments from the reefs, producing a constant build-up of fine sand, whose hallmark is the pink flecking created by tiny corals and shells.

Although Horseshoe Bay is perhaps the most widely known of the island's beaches, it is quite erroneous to assume that this one alone stands out for its natural beauty. Indeed, one of the remarkable things about Bermuda's beaches is that there are so many of them, with small, secluded coves scattered between the larger beaches, each possessing its own unique charm. Readily accessible from public roadways and bus routes are the main beaches at Warwick Long Bay, John Smith's Bay, Chaplin Bay, Jobson's Cove and Horseshoe Bay. Each of these, plus numerous others that intermittently line the South Shore, can be reached by walking down from the main road and wandering through miles of sand dunes. In addition, most of the hotels along this expanse of coast have their own private beach – although all are ostensibly public below low tide, providing that no trespassing is required to access them.

At the East End – and equally as stunning – are Clearwater Beach, Tobacco Bay, Achilles Bay and Fort St Catherine's Beach, where the backdrop is the formidable walls of a nineteenth-century fortification. Just a ten-minute drive away

from St George westwards along Ferry Reach Road is the rather under-used beach at Whale Bone Bay, while nestled along the north-facing shoreline is a quiet area sometimes used as an authorized summer campsite by Bermudians seeking to enjoy the peace and solitude of the surrounding parkland.

SHIPWRECKS

It was reputedly Sir Walter Raleigh who initially sounded the clarion horn to warn seafarers that the Bermudas were dangerous and should be avoided at all costs. Bermuda, indeed, has always been a natural hazard to shipping on account of its extensive and complex reefs. Outside the south reef, where the water almost immediately drops straight down into the unfathomable depths of the Atlantic Ocean, unknown numbers of ill-fated mariners have met their doom. Elsewhere, however, dozens of wrecks have been located, identified and researched.

One of the oldest wrecks is, of course, the *Sea Venture*, which hit a reef off Fort St Catherine's Beach in July 1609. The sunken ship was severely cannibalized by its passengers and crew, who supplemented their salvage with locally found cedar trees and built themselves two smaller vessels, in which they completed their journey to Jamestown, Virginia. Four centuries later, the remnants of this shipwreck resemble a scattered cadaver encrusted with dense coral

Above Encircled by reefs, the intermingling of shallow sandy beds and outcrops of coral has provided Bermuda's waterscape with a stunning range of blues and radiant turquoise.

Opposite Fully intact, sitting upright in crystal-clear water, the Hermes is considered Bermuda's most popular wreck dive.

growth; only a marine archaeologist could help to make its shape discernible.

But the wrecks of other vessels remain much more in tact, for example the *San Antonio*, which came to grief on 12 September 1621. A splendid Spanish galleon sailing under Captain Fernandino da Vera, the vessel had been making its way from Cartagena to Cadiz with a treasure trove of gold and silver destined for the Royal Court in Madrid.

Falling victim to the north reef, she lies in that same spot to this day, a haven for marine life and curious human onlookers. Three decades later, in 1658, the English merchant ship *Eagle* met a similar fate. Owned by the Virginia Company, and making what should have been a routine passage between England and Jamestown, the ship sunk when Captain George Withy misjudged the proximity of a coral outcrop. Within hours, ship and cargo were settled into the sandy bottom where they continue to gently rot and decay.

Ironically, *HMS Cerebus* was actually departing from Bermuda when she foundered. Leaving rather too hastily from anchorage in St George in order to hunt down a pirate vessel reported to have been seen close by, Captain Parkingson inadvertently wrecked his ship just off Castle Island in February 1783. Although the crew survived, this elegant Royal Navy battleship sank below the waves, complete with all 32 guns that were carried aboard.

There are countless other stories to be gleaned from Bermuda's rich maritime history, in which innocents have often found themselves forever condemned to these ocean graveyards. The Confederate paddle-steamer *Marie Celeste* sank off Church Bay in 1864, her cargo of rifles destined for Savannah leaving a trail among coral outcrops. *SS Pollockshields* spectacularly came to rest just off Elbow Beach during the hurricane of 1915. She had been heavily laden with weaponry and munitions for the Bermuda Garrison. The Spanish passenger steamer *Cristobal Colon* struck each of North Rock in 1936. At 10,600 tons, she became the largest vessel ever to be wrecked in Bermuda.

Buried by sand, or broken up and coated with

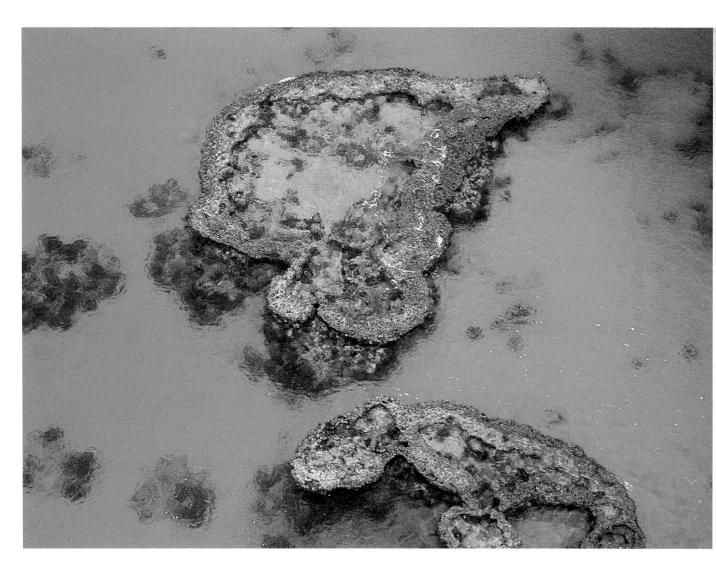

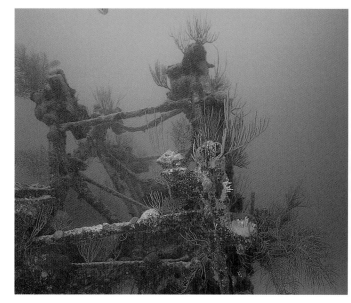

coral, wrecks have gradually become integrated into the reef system, providing homes for all manner of sea life. Sharks glide about their hulls, fish swim through the spars and moray eels lurk deep within shattered hatches and stairwells. Unauthorized diving of wreck sites is discouraged and their desecration is strictly illegal. However, the Bermuda Government does issue permits to licensed scuba operators.

Opposite Reefs known as 'boilers' occur on the southern and southeastern side of the island. They are small, generally rounded reefs that extend to the sea surface and waves continuously break over them.

Opposite left Portuguese-Man-of-War are frequently seen in Bermuda waters. These blue jelly fish have fiercely stinging, food-catching tentacles up to fifty metres (nearly 140 feet) long.

Opposite right The Marie Celeste, a high-speed, side-paddlewheel steamer, sank in 1864 after hitting a reef close to Bermuda's south shore.

Above For nearly 500 years, ships have run aground on the treacherous reefs that surround Bermuda. As a result, the island holds the title of 'Shipwreck Capital of the Atlantic'.

Page 56-57 Spectacular sunsets such as this are common sights throughout the year. The clarity of the Bermuda air, and the low landscape horizon make them visible from most parts of the island.

Culture

Visitors tend to generalize about Bermuda and regard it as being 'quaintly British'. In reality, it enjoys a culture that is significantly more expansive. With a population base dominated by people descended from Afro-West Indian backgrounds, the Portuguese Azores Islands and the United Kingdom, the island's culture is the result of a subtle merger of each of these differing roots. Contemporary Bermudian society has also been injected with ideas and cultures from elsewhere in the world as workers have arrived from diverse parts of the globe.

FUSION OF CULTURES

To some extent, the diversity within Bermuda is reflected in the variety of religions represented here. Bermuda is officially an Anglican community, but many other Christian denominations are represented, including Baptists – who sometimes conduct full-immersion services at secluded beaches – Evangelicals, Roman Catholics, Seventh-Day Adventists, Lutherans, African Methodist Episcopalians and Scottish Presbyterians. Muslims have a mosque in Hamilton, while the Ethiopian Orthodox Church has its own centre, as do Christian Scientists and those of the Bahá'i faith. Hindus have private multiple-deity altars in their homes. Jews, Rosicrucians and Rastafarians add to the rich religious culture, each group lending its own codes of dress and conduct – as well as specific rites, processions and days of celebration – to Bermuda's cultural fabric.

Above The port of Hamilton thrives on shipping activity. However, the city is also the focal-point of Bermuda's international business community.

Right The Bermuda Government Aquarium, in Flatts, displays only local fish and marine life. There is an adjacent Natural History Museum and thematic Zoo.

During May of each year 'Heritage Month' is dedicated to recognizing various elements of the islands' cultural mosaic. Schools conduct activities focusing on aspects of Bermuda's diversity, radio and television programmes explore its history, grandparents reminisce about earlier times and sporting legends relive their moments of glory. The seventeenth-century St Peter's Church in St George may recall its origin as the island's first church, while Cobb's Hill Church might remind its congregation that the original building was erected by freed slaves. Individual sports and workingmen's clubs sometimes stage their own special events. Collectively, such activities generate an awareness of the past that might otherwise be forgotten, while also helping to promote an interest in their roots among those of the younger generations.

The highlight of Heritage Month is the parade that takes place in Hamilton on 24 May. To some extent this was born of a previous tradition known as the Floral Pageant, when a succession of floats decorated with flowers and foliage annually wound its way along Front Street. Today the procession has been expanded considerably to include steel bands, troupes of majorettes, dancers, cyclists and school and service floats. It commences in Hamilton and meanders its way through the streets until ending either in Bernard Park or the National Sports Centre, where an open party of music, food and dancing continues well into the night.

Above Situated at the end of Hamilton Harbour, The Bermuda Underwater Research Institute contains numerous exhibits outlining Bermuda's seafaring heritage. Of special interest is a definitive shell collection in one of the main galleries.

Opposite Some of the highlights of the Botanical Gardens include the palm garden with native palmetto trees, the subtropical fruit garden and the garden for the blind, featuring scented plants and the ficus collection.

CREATIVE ARTS

Bermuda has a very active arts scene. The Bermuda National Gallery, the Art Centre at Dockyard and the Bermuda Society of Arts provide venues for regular exhibitions of painting and sculpture by Bermudian and guest artists alike. In a secluded gallery in the Botanical Gardens, the Masterworks Foundation maintains a collection of repatriated paintings that have been created by artists from overseas. Private commercial galleries and artists' studios also abound.

Between April and late September, open-air street festivals are held in St George and Hamilton, each showcasing a selection of local arts and crafts, as well as food stalls and live entertainment. Amateur theatrical groups ensure that the theatre-goers of Bermuda are kept occupied throughout the year and there is an annual Christmas pantomime to entertain young and old alike.

The Bermuda Music Festival, held in early autumn, attracts international entertainers in the fields of jazz, pop and soul, as well as other musical genres. The Winter Festival, held during January and February each year, features art forms ranging from live theatre to dancing and music. Bermuda also boasts a very successful International Film Festival, during which it plays host to cinematographers from around the world.

Opposite Much of Bermuda grinds to a halt for two days every summer while the Cup Match Cricket game is on. As well as cricket, dancing and other festivities also take place on this National Holiday first celebrated in 1947.

Left A legacy from days of British rule, Hot Cross Buns are an Easter treat either available from bakeries or home-made. The cross on the bun represents Christ's agony and death on the cross.

Below The Nature Reserve at Spittal Pond is an ideal place to enjoy watching for both migrant and resident birds. Also to be found here is 'Spanish Rock', a carving thought to have been made by a shipwrecked sailor in 1543.

Opposite left A scuba diving chef, complete with frying pan, is not what you might expect to see in the Bermuda Aquarium. You can however count on viewing 200 species of local fish, marine turtles and harbour seals.

Opposite top Palm Grove is famous for its pond, which features a relief map of Bermuda in the middle. On the map, each parish is an immaculately manicured grassy division. The site, which has well-landscaped flower gardens, opens onto a view of the sea.

Opposite bottom The Bermuda Regiment Band performs at official occasions such as the Queen's birthday parade.

Above left and right Born of a blend of African, West Indian and North American Indian cultures, Gombey dance troupes provide a truly unique exposure to the magic of local folklore. The troupe comprises of 10 to 30 dancers, usually all men. The dance is traditionally performed at Christmas and Easter.

Left 18th century Verdmont, in Smith's Parish, enables visitors to personally experience the grandeur of the period. Owned by the Bermuda National Trust, it is one of many similar properties that is open to the public on a regular basis. Each of the rooms has been carefully preserved, so as to quickly allow visitors to slip into an era of long ago.

Above This is a replica of the *Deliverance*, one of two vessels built by the survivors of the *Sea Venture* when it was shipwrecked in 1609. Accompanied by the *Patience*, both boats finally managed to complete the voyage to Jamestown, Virginia, one year later.

Sports and Activities

The subtropical climate that Bermudians enjoy throughout the year has made outdoor sporting activities a natural pastime. Most recognized sports – both water and land based – thrive here. From surfboarding, swimming, waterskiing, windsurfing, canoeing and deep-sea fishing to football, cricket, rugby, field hockey and netball, most sporting activities have an organized following. The same is true of indoor sports, which include everything from martial arts and boxing to darts, squash and bodybuilding. Equestrian events and pony racing occur in two customized arenas.

NATIONAL SPORTS

Football and cricket are both enthusiastically played locally through league and knockout tournaments; each is also avidly followed overseas. Both games have dominated community grounds and fields from one end of the country to the other for longer than anyone can remember. Cricket is played from May to August, while the football season spans the remainder of the year. Both embrace all age groups and there are always sufficient players to engage numerous teams in competitive matches.

In cricket, which is regulated nationally by the Bermuda Cricket Board of Control, the traditional highlight of the season is the annual Cup Match Classic, when a team representing St George competes against its counterpart from Somerset in an end-to-end rivalry that reaches back more than a century. If Bermuda has a national party, then this two-day cricket fiesta must surely be it. Cup

Above Bermuda has a world-wide reputation as a golfing paradise.

Opposite Aquatic options include windsurfing, kayaking or canoeing, which can be enjoyed in one of the many tranquil inlets or bays around the islands.

Above top Mid-Ocean is universally recognised as being one of the most prestigious and attractive golf course in the world.

Above The public golf course at St. George's is one of the most picturesque and enjoyable on the island.

__Above top__ Playing and watching cricket is a very popular pastime. The highlight of the season is the annual Cup Match, played between two of the island's leading clubs – Somerset and St. George's.

Match is an officially designated Public Holiday marked by closed shops and offices and modified bus and ferry services. There are food stalls, fashion parades, tented campsites and music, and even gambling gets a tacit nod with 'Crown and Anchor' boards attracting scores of players, ensuring that lots of cash rapidly changes hands. Out on the pitch, under the glare of the hot sun, the cricketers steadfastly bat, bowl and field their way from morning to dusk with intermittent breaks for water, slices of orange, lunch and tea. The winners are awarded

Above top Cricket is one of the island's national sports, and attracts an enthusiastic following of players and spectators.

Above The Annual Rugby Classic offers sporting enthusiasts the opportunity to watch international teams from around the world, competing for the Bermuda Bowl.

Opposite Avid snorkellers can always find places of fascination and enjoyment virtually anywhere along the shoreline.

the treasured trophy – and then spend the next couple of days driving across the countryside in a self-congratulatory victory cavalcade. This remarkable passion for cricket also takes Bermudian fans to the West Indies, England and Australia to watch International Test Matches.

Football has a similar following of devoted players and supporters. There are multiple divisions to accommodate all levels of talent, age and commitment, with friendly and league games scheduled for each weekend during the season. An all-encompassing knockout tournament climaxes with the local Cup Final being played at the National Sports Centre in Devonshire. Bermuda has always done well in this sport on the international stage. Representative teams have participated quite successfully in early regional rounds of the World Cup, while the national squad won the silver medal in the Commonwealth Games of 1966. Several individual players have gone on to enjoy successful professional careers overseas: Clyde Best (West Ham) and Shaun Goater (Manchester City) are just two young Bermudians to have left their mark while playing with English Premiership teams.

Despite the often oppressive humidity, road-running has a remarkably dedicated following of active participants and passive supporters. There is a regular calendar of events for enthusiasts – as indeed there is for triathlon and other athletic events – with two highlights dominating the year. In late January Bermuda hosts International Race Weekend, which attracts hundreds of overseas runners to these shores to participate in a series of five races ranging from the 'Front Street Mile' to a full marathon. Top-level athletes from the

colder regions of Europe and North America find that the conditions here merge perfectly with their pre-season warm-ups prior to the launch of various international competitions. For most Bermudians, however, the athletic highlight of the year is probably the 'Bermuda Day Marathon', which has been held for decades on 24 May each year. Personal success in this special event, which is technically neither a full nor a half marathon, is the goal of most local road-runners and the male and female victors are accepted as Bermuda's crowned champions.

Inevitably, sailing is also a major activity. There are several major clubs based at St George, Somerset, Hamilton and Spanish Point, each of which organizes extensive development pro-grammes for young sailors as well as scheduling a summer calendar for competitive crews. With most international classes represented – and Bermudians holding world rankings in most

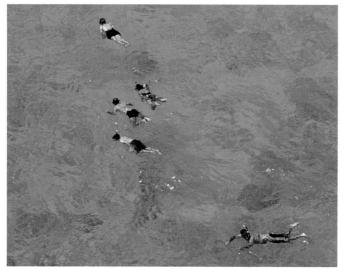

and titles in some – it could be that emotional attention focuses on the unique Bermuda Fitted Dinghy. This extraordinary racer is distinctive for carrying what most would regard as an inordinate volume of sail for such a relatively small hull. Designed a century ago specifically for local inshore sailing, there is nowhere else in the world where these boats can be seen. There is a surviving fleet of 10 or so with the potential to participate in the season's list of races, but perhaps only a handful of these have made it into the water in recent years. The season

officially commences at St George on 24 May with a series of races in the harbour. With colouful spinnakers billowing and crew members strategically jumping overboard in order to lighten the load, this remarkable spectacle attracts shoreline spectators and an abundance of very vocal followers aboard congested water traffic.

For visitors eager to participate in guided snorkelling tours, scuba diving, water-skiing, hang-gliding and jet-skiing, there are several commercial companies owned and operated by Bermudians that can accommodate most requirements. Likewise, local businesses provide glass-bottom boat trips, catamaran excursions and charter fishing with an expert guide. Of course, direct access to all sports and related activities can always be made by contacting the appropriate clubs and associations listed in the telephone directory.

Opposite top Originally formed in 1844, the Royal Bermuda Yacht Club has occupied these premises since they were built in the 1930s. It is the co-host for the Newport-Bermuda Ocean Yacht Race.

Opposite bottom Surrounded by clean, crystal waters, young Bermudians have traditionally been fascinated by life beneath the surface.

Above With many shipwrecks settled around the island, as well as numerous caves and exceptional coral reefs, Bermuda is a diver's paradise. There are several different companies on the islands offering dive instruction, equipment rental and guided excursions.

Above Fishing from shore, as well as deep-sea fishing, is popular with both locals and tourists alike.

Opposite top The St.George's Dinghy and Sports Club hosts local and visiting yachtsmen. Nearby is the smaller but equally important East End Mini Yacht Club, which has a thriving youth development programme.

Opposite bottom The Crown and Anchor game is a gambling game traditionally played on the Cup Match National Holiday. The board consists of six sections, each with a symbol: crown, anchor, diamond, club, heart and spade. These symbols correspond to those on the dice. Players bet on which symbol they think the 'banker' will roll; they can win as much as three times the amount of their stake, depending on how many selected symbols turn up. If no selection appears, you lose your stake.

Left International Race Week in Bermuda draws over 250 American, British, Canadian, European skippers and crew to Bermuda. The races are held during April/May each year.

Above Many couples travel to Bermuda in order to get married. The water's edge at Astwood Cove is a popular venue.

In memory of David F. Raine, who died five weeks after completing this book. David had eighteen books published and this last book, *The Magic of Bermuda* reflects his love of his island home, Bermuda.

First published in 2005 by
New Holland Publishers Ltd
London • Cape Town • Sydney • Auckland

www.newhollandpublishers.com

Garfield House, 86–88 Edgware Road, London W2 2EA, United Kingdom

80 McKenzie Street, Cape Town 8001, South Africa

14 Aquatic Drive, Frenchs Forest, NSW 2086, Australia

218 Lake Road, Northcote, Auckland, New Zealand

ISBN 1 84330 939 4

Publishing Manager: Jo Hemmings
Senior Editor: Charlotte Judet
Designer: Tyrone Taylor
Production: Joan Woodroffe
Cartographer: William Smuts

Reproduction by Pica Digital Pte Ltd, Singapore
Printed & bound in Singapore by Tien Wah Press (Pte) Ltd

PHOTOGRAPHIC CREDITS

Front Cover: St. George's waterfront; Back Cover: Gombey Dancers; Page 1: Harrington Sound; Page 80: Nonsuch Island .
All images © Bermuda Department of Tourism except: p 12, 28(br), 34(b), 38, 44(tl), 62, 63(t, b), 64(l), 68, 71, 77 © Bermuda Royal Gazette; p7(b), 8, 9(t,b), 10(t,b), 15(t, bl, br), 17(b), 18(t), 20(t), 22(tl,b), 25(r), 26(t, b), 27(t), 28(tl, tr, bl), 31(b), 32(t), 33, 34(t), 35, 36, 37, 40, 41, 42(tl, tr, c), 44(tr), 45(b), 54(bl), 56, 77(t), 79 © Jill Amos Raine; 4, 7(b), 8, 45(t), 46(tl, tr, bl, br), 48, 53, 54(br, t), 55, 75 © Lawson Wood.